SEVENTEEN
COME SUNDAY

SEVENTEEN
COME SUNDAY

A Birthday Letter

BY
RUTH ROBINSON

THE WESTMINSTER PRESS
PHILADELPHIA

Photographs
by
R. A. BEEM
Newton Highlands
Massachusetts

LIBRARY OF CONGRESS CATALOG CARD No. 67–12089

Published by The Westminster Press®
Philadelphia, Pennsylvania

PRINTED IN THE UNITED STATES OF AMERICA

CONTENTS

PREFACE TO THE READER

THIS BOOK was written in the first instance for
one person, my daughter Catherine. It is an attempt
to express a stage in a discussion that has been develop-
ing over the past seventeen years and so was, in one
sense, written just as much for myself as for her. It
represents, if you like, the point to which the questionings, promptings and response of my children have
brought me and is therefore in the nature of a dialogue
between the generations. It is because we are sure that
there is much misunderstanding and great longing for
communication between parents and children in Christian households that we are glad to share the dialogue
with others, in case it may indicate for you, too, at
what points communication is possible.

You should not then think that I was writing for
some extraordinarily precocious sixth-former. Those
who know her will not recognize Catherine in this
role. It happens that she and I have learnt to share
what you might call the same language of thinking, so

that she may perhaps more readily recognize what it is, in terms of personal experience and response, that I am struggling to express. I am really writing for any parent who may find himself secretly questioning ways of expressing belief which he has been happy with for years, precisely because, despite all that may have been shared together, his children are unable to accept these ways for themselves. I am writing for any child who respects and longs to share the spiritual depth and vitality he recognizes in his parents but is unable to accept their terms with integrity. I am writing for anyone on either side of the generation divide, whether parent, child, teacher or student, who would like to find a way of engaging in real dialogue across it. It is a question of getting beneath the level of outward structure, whether of dogma, religious observance or institution, to a reality which all can share and recognize.

Perhaps, in order to illustrate the intensity of the problem at the point where it is most keenly felt, I can allow my younger fourteen-year-old daughter to express it for herself. She had been asked to write a Scripture essay on what she thought about God and, in a subsequent discussion, to say how she would talk about God to a small child. She began the essay by saying firmly: ' I don't believe in God for a start. I think it is all in the mind.' She went on to explain that she thinks God is your conscience: a voice inside telling you what sort of a person you ought to be. (This for an adult Christian may be inadequate but it represents what is real for her now in her own experience and is therefore a growing point.)

On the question of talking about God to a child she revealed what I can only describe as a genuine anger. She says she doesn't know how you *can* talk about God to a child without causing it to misunderstand. ' How can a child not think God is an actual person in a place called Heaven, when everyone talks about him as " Him." Even in church, *where you expect them to tell the truth*, they pray to him as if he were a person and even put him where you can see him in stained glass windows.' She says she first realized all this was ' stupid ' when she began to understand about space and rockets and then, she says, ' you don't know what to think. You feel you have been cheated with fairy-stories which the grown-ups still apparently believe and, at the same time, you feel guilty because you can't believe them yourself.'

She now finds herself at the point where she is beginning to understand that the grown-ups *don't* believe this, nor did they expect her to believe it in this literal way. It has all been a complete misunderstanding. Her final, bitter cri-de-coeur should be writ large before the eyes of any of us who presume to be involved in ' religious instruction ' whether at home or in school: ' But you just think of all those years when I *thought* I didn't believe in God! '

This, then, is the living context of this book, the point at which misunderstanding must be exposed and communication attempted. The child's dilemma, moreover, helps me to express a similar difficulty I found in writing my third chapter on the Church. For just as she is torn between a commitment to the spiritual values she shares with her parents, and her inability to identify herself with the form in which they are expressed, so do I find myself torn between respect for and sympathy with the lively and committed Christians in our churches, many of whom are my friends, and lack of enthusiasm for so much of the activity in which they are involved. But if I seem to speak negatively about the religious organization, it is because I feel positively about the community of Holy Spirit, for this holds my greater loyalty. And even where I speak critically, I am myself involved within the criticism, not judging from outside.

Nevertheless, I recognize regretfully that some of what I say may hurt or bewilder those who do not share or understand my doubts about organized religion. I can only say, firstly, that I am writing for those who *do* share them and, secondly, that it may sometimes be more loving, and I would think less condescending, to speak openly knowing it may hurt, than to keep silent simply from fear of hurting.

I wrote primarily, as I have said, for Catherine's sake, because I was concerned to help her towards some expression of her spiritual perceptions which she could genuinely and honestly recognize as relevant, before she found herself abandoning the Christian framework altogether. This concern is extended to all who share, perhaps with similar discomfort, our frontier position. If you don't share it, I hope you will nevertheless be able to accept the integrity of my concern and to discern the Spirit which has prompted it.

RUTH ROBINSON

FOREWORD

[To be sung *con spirito*]

How old are you, my fair pretty maid?
How old are you, my honey?
She answered me right cheerfully:
I am seventeen come Sunday.
With my rue dum day, fol the diddle dol,
Fol the dol the diddle dum the day.

— *Folk song from Somerset,*
where you were born.

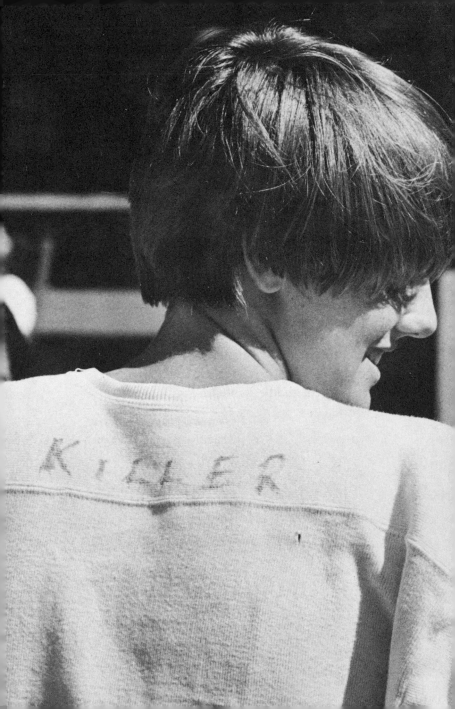

January 31st, 1966

Dear Catherine,

You will think this a very odd sort of birthday letter so I must explain it. What I am going to try and share with you has been simmering in my mind for some time. It could simmer, I suppose, indefinitely until it shared the fate of all simmering pots and dried up. But I must stir myself and bring it to the boil, and your approaching birthday provides the stimulus and date-line that I need. So here I am, as it were, turning up the gas and setting the pinger for February 10th!

You and I have shared many Saturday evening depressions over the last year as we viewed the prospect of the next day's ' boring services and crummy sermons ' — your quote. We felt we had a commitment, we knew we must respond to it, we wanted to acknowledge and express it, but not like this. We have sung hymns and recited words which were not merely wide of the mark but sickeningly so, that at times they seemed a distortion and even a degradation of the commitment we were longing to meet. We have confessed before Communion that the burden of our misdoings is intolerable, we have stated, after absolution, that we are still unworthy to gather up the crumbs; and after this glorious feast, this Messianic banquet, we have still gone on begging for mercy. No wonder we have felt as we left our seats: ' This is where I came in.'

But what, we have wondered, about the ' eager expectation ' with which the created universe is waiting? What about the ' harvest of the Spirit ' — love, joy, peace? We can't settle for anything less and the crumbs are no longer enough. We have felt hungry and frustrated and, in consequence, have had less to give.

And there is more to it than that. Mouths are for speaking as well as for eating and we have been discomforted by words. The Sunday words have bothered us; words like grace, redemption, atonement — the lip-service we pay each week, like half-crowns into the collection plate. But there are also other coins which have seemed far more vital to our ordinary day-to-day spiritual subsistence and which no longer seem to have the purchasing power they once had — words like God, Christ, Holy Spirit. The reality is there, constantly claiming us, but the coins, the words, can somehow no longer be exchanged. Sometimes it seems as though we were trying to conduct a world economy on the basis of cowrie shells.

So we have sympathized with those, and the younger clergy are not least among them, who have said they are finding it increasingly difficult to use this ' God-language ' in their sermons. We have sympathized even more when their seniors have responded with a rueful shake of the head and seemed to suggest that ' poor so-and-so has lost his faith.' Lost his faith indeed! To lose one's faith is to be bereft of all that gives meaning and purpose to life, as people feel at the death of a close relative, and this would be blackness indeed. But this is far from the case of many who are raising questions about ' God-language.' They raise them precisely because it matters so much that the language should measure up to the commitment that claims them. The mood is one of discovery, not loss, of trust, not despair.

What I am going to try and share with you is an exploration along the frontiers of religious language. If, during the course of it, we learn to *recognize* the frontier when we get there and to know when we have reached the point where language can carry us no further, that in itself will be something. For it will give us a greater freedom this side of the frontier. We shall then be able to walk with trust and discrimination, more able to spot and avoid those places where we are likely to get bogged down in language, go round in circles or wander up dead ends. We may even come to move with trust across the frontier, though there will be no language to observe or record such a happening. Our only identification will be to live among our fellows, as those who, while they respect and value language in its proper sphere, are able to pass freely and trustfully across its frontiers.

What I write will have to be brief — it is only ten days till your birthday.[1] But this is all to the good. I can't go far with you in any case. All I can do is to set you on the way of your own quest. It comes with my love for your birthday in the hope, as you live through the year of being seventeen, that it may provide a little spiritual income to draw on, even if immediate funds, come Sunday, sometimes seem low!

Your loving and grateful

M.

---

[1] I did, as you know, only manage two of my three chapters, in amongst feeding the family, in time for the day itself. The third was promised during the next week and was in fact finished on the morning of Stephen's eighteenth birthday (while he was at choir practice and compulsory college chapel!). He and I talked a long time on the evening before, so he has been very much in on it too!

1

THE PRIMARY WORD

SOME time ago, just before Christmas, I found un-expectedly that I had a day to myself. Something put in my mind a book that I first read twenty-one years ago, which then made a tremendous impression on me, as it did on many of my generation. This was Martin Buber's *I and Thou* — a sort of prose poem, part philosophy, part mysticism. You would have to read it for yourself in order to savour its distinctive quality.

I took the book from the shelf and looked, as a stranger, at my maiden name on the fly-leaf with the date: ' June 1944.' It seemed like a different world, a different age. I flicked over the pages, noticing the places I had marked in the margin, and wondered whether I would mark the same things now; what indeed I would make of it at all.

I supposed I should find it very dated and rather touchingly old-fashioned, just as we feel when we turn up an old photograph: Did we ever think those clothes were attractive or that hair-style becoming? (While at the same time we remember rather affectionately what it felt like to be us when we did!) I expected it would be like that with Buber. *I–Thou* has become a sort of cliché, an accepted truism that everyone takes for granted. The point no longer needs to be laboured.

The day was before me, so I sat down and began to read from the beginning with a sort of nostalgic curiosity, thinking that, in a while, I would put it away again and forget it for another twenty years. I did put it down once or twice to brew up another cup of coffee, but I read through to the end and it was like a revelation — just as it was the first time but utterly different.

My first reaction was one of amazement. How could it have meant so much to me all those years ago — I had obviously understood so little of it? The answer is that I was asking different questions the first time, and it was these questions that Buber had answered in an illuminating way. Where he spoke to what vitally concerned me then, the book came to me as revelation, though there was also a lot more that I accepted readily with the top of my mind as ' a good way of putting it ' but which yet lay outside my close concern. But now the things that I formerly accepted so readily have a new urgency about them, so that what then seemed a good way of putting it now speaks as revelation. It is a matter of where you are most deeply involved.

When I first read it, it was personal relationship that most nearly concerned us. The war was still on; millions had been killed or exterminated in gas chambers. It was vitally important to distinguish between treating people as persons with real value and dignity, meeting one with an inescapable claim, and making use of them as functions or manipulating them as objects. Relationship to God was also important but we didn't agonize over it; it seemed to be a natural implication of the depth of our human relationships. God himself seemed relatively secure and not in question. In those days, or at any rate, later in the 1940s, we were active in the parishes stimulating discussion groups on the recently published document: *Towards the Conversion of England*!

This isn't an entirely true picture because I can see, looking back, that already the questionings and promptings that stir us now were germinating then. In 1944, John Robinson was putting the finishing touches to a lengthy doctorate thesis, never yet published, on the doctrine of God, with special reference to Buber's *I and Thou*. It was called *Thou Who Art*, which would then have been recognized in theological circles as an oblique thrust at an existing title, *He Who*

Is, by Dr Mascall. The same protagonists are still active on the same front but there hardly seems a chance of them engaging to any purpose: their weapons are so different. One day, I must get out that thesis and dust it.

But I want to share with you what I have found in Buber's book, reading it again.

Let me first try and describe what the spiritual scene looks like for me, standing where I do, and then see what light Buber sheds on it. The view may be different from where you stand, but between us we may get it in perspective.

There are various ways of describing the scene from where I am. It is as if there were some defect of vision so that the image from each eye weren't exactly super-imposed; each picture is clear separately but they just don't fit. Sometimes I have the impression of a schizo-phrenic existence, of living in two worlds at once, one of which is completely unintelligible to the other. This is precisely the effect of the snide question: 'How can you pray to the Ground of your being?' There seems no common mode in which to attempt an answer.

You may know the story of the two explorers and the clearing where there were many flowers growing. One said some gardener must tend it; the other said there was no gardener at all. It ended with the sceptic wanting to know what was the difference between ' an invisible, intangible, eternally elusive gardener ' and an imaginary one or no gardener at all. Here, I stand wholeheartedly with the sceptic; I am ready to assert straight off: ' There *is* no gardener ' without all these qualifications. At the same time, ' My Lord and my God,' in its own context, holds echoes of a claim upon me which is recognizable and inescapable. So I find myself among those who are accused of wanting to have their cake and eat it.

What Buber does for me in this situation is to provide a pair of spectacles which adjusts the vision, if one can apply so prosaic a metaphor to such an elusive and provocative book.

He describes the two ways in which I can be in relation to the world that confronts me, whether to persons or to things, to nature or to art, or ultimately to ' God.' I can be involved in the relation of *I* to *Thou* in a direct reciprocal way, so that I am, in my whole being, *within* the relationship and cannot step outside it and observe it without destroying it. This, as it were, corresponds to the world of the vocative, the second person singular. In this case the ' other ' stands over against me and we are mutually *in* relation, in the same way as we talk about two people being ' in ' love. Or I can be involved as an *I* to an *It*, in which case the ' other ' is part of my self-conscious world, something to be observed, talked about, acted upon. This you might call the world of the third person — he, she, it or they.

So already, at the outset, I can recognize the outline of my dilemma; perhaps my double vision is an advantage, not a hindrance. Buber's opening sentence states quite simply and directly: ' To man the world is twofold, in accordance with his twofold attitude.' This statement gives me hope. Perhaps I am meant to see double!

For Buber, these two combinations *I–Thou* and *I–It, He or She* are what he calls the two primary words. In all my relationships and all my attitudes I am, moment by moment, speaking one of these primary words. Moreover, the *I* of the *I–Thou* combination is a different *I* from that of the *I–It* combination. When I say *I–Thou* I say it with my whole being because I am taking my stand in relation; I am wholly committed. When I say, *I–It*, I have detached myself from relationship and stand outside, regarding, observing. I can never say *I–It* with my *whole* being; I am then, as it were, acting a part, a part of me.

I don't want to appear to be adding another chapter in the Pooh-Perplex series, but there is a sort of parable of this in Rabbit's attempt in *Winnie-the-Pooh* to evade a direct encounter with his visitor. Pooh begins:

' Hallo, Rabbit, isn't that you? '

' No,' said Rabbit in a different sort of voice this
  time.

' But isn't that Rabbit's voice? '

' I don't *think* so,' said Rabbit. ' It isn't meant to
  be.' . . .

' Well, could you very kindly tell me where Rabbit
  is? '

' He has gone to see his friend Pooh Bear, who is a
  great friend of his.'

' But this *is* Me! ' said Bear, much surprised.

' What sort of Me? '

' Pooh Bear.'

' Are you sure? ' said Rabbit, still more surprised.

' Quite, quite sure,' said Pooh.

' Oh well, then, come in.' . . .

' You were quite right,' said Rabbit looking at him
  all over. ' It *is* you. Glad to see you.'

You can see how ' Glad to see you ' introduces a
quite different ' feel.' Rabbit is at last being himself
instead of acting a part, and they can talk to each other
directly instead of in the third person. I know I can't
really explain to you the difference between these two
modes of relating; you will only understand if you
' feel.' the difference for yourself.

Buber shows how this difference comes to light in
the spiritual history both of primitive man and the
new-born child. The speech of primitive man indicates
a relationship, whereas civilized speech is much more

indirect and abstracted. Compare, for example, the ever-fresh Kaffir greeting, with its direct bodily relation, ' I see you ' with our conventional and polite ' How do you do? '

A new-born child has no conscious awareness of himself as *I*. At first there is simply a ' rapport ' with what is over against him; his whole being is in the reaching out to the other. ' These very glances will after protracted attempts settle on the red carpet-pattern and not be moved till the soul of the red has opened itself to them.' ' Little, disjointed, meaningless sounds still go out persistently into the void. But one day, unforeseen, they will have become conversation — does it matter that it is perhaps with the simmering kettle? ' He only becomes conscious of himself as *I* after he has learnt consciously to discriminate between objects in the exterior world. The *Thou* separates itself into teddy bear, Mummy, Daddy, then: ' Johnny's teddy bear, Johnny's Mummy, Johnny's Daddy,' until ' Johnny,' then ' Me ' and finally ' I ' stands alone, observing and testing the world outside him. He is then able to say ' I love my teddy '; but what a world of difference lies between this and the ' movement of the hands (which) will win from a woolly teddy bear its precise form, apparent to the senses, and become lovingly and unforgettably aware of a complete body.' To be sure, the ' memory ' of the earlier complete relatedness haunts the later words, 'I love Teddy,' filling the experience of loving with an unutterable yearning; but the words themselves, and even the feeling, are no more than a shadow, a flat projection.

There is something of the same difference between a map — which is also a sort of projection — and the countryside in which I am standing and of which, at the moment of being here, I am a living part. Think of a map of America, for example. Some maps are rather primitive and not very exact or reliable by modern standards, though they often manage to give an intriguing impression of what it must have been like to live there at the time maps were made: 'Buffalo swamp,' 'Elephants' bones found here,' 'Wandering Indians and man-eaters,' 'Here Mr de la Salle was killed in 1687.' In many ways the old maps are more evocative of the living scene than our more modern, scientific ones, though the latter give us more exact information about the structure. In these, vegetation, population, rainfall, temperature, are all laid out before us, and the country is clearly set out for us as Canadian Shield, Great Plains, Colorado Plateau, Great Basin. But when all is said, the map is still no more than a piece of paper printed in colour, reflecting second-hand images in our mind.

Think now, instead, of the eeriness of travelling

across that vast salt desert, with those miles and miles of cracked dried mud and sage brush and the fantastic yellow cliffs of a one-time sea. Remember Jenny Lake at six o'clock in the morning: the smell of the pines as we trod down the needles and shuffled through the cones, the sudden light on the white birches, the occasional brief shape of an unfamiliar animal, the sound of the hidden waterfall we were determined to find. We were *part* of that scene; no map could reproduce it in its completeness, for it would show none of these things, nor the urgency and sadness of a last morning in a place we knew we might never see again. We may look and look at a map, and try to recapture the event in words, but nothing measures up to being literally ' in the picture ' ourselves.

This seems to me to be just the difference between being aware of God and talking about ' him ' or trying to describe our experience of ' him.' If you ask me: ' How can you pray to the Ground of your being? ' I might answer: ' How can the Great Basin send a shiver down your spine? ' You can't meet a *Thou* under the terms of *It*.

All language about God, whether theological or religious, in textbooks or in worship, belongs to the world of *It*. God is the purpose, the point, the object of the language; while he is that he is never my *Thou*, even when I call him *Thou* with my lips. ' When

Thou is spoken ' (spoken by the whole being, that is, in Buber's sense of ' speaking ') ' the speaker has no thing for his object.' (There *is* no gardener.) ' When *Thou* is spoken, the speaker has no *thing;* he has indeed nothing. But he takes his stand in relation.'

We must, nevertheless, use the language of words and ideas to describe and communicate what we have known, just as we need to use maps of America. As in the case of the maps, the earlier, more primitive words often seem to have more life about them because they are so clearly the direct reflection of immediate encounter. Jacob's wrestling-bout, Elijah's still small voice, Isaiah's live coal, Jesus' ' Abba, Father,' all these speak to us because we recognize something of the relationship they describe. Later words and ideas, developed into doctrine and theology, may be more detailed and exhaustive and in some ways more instructive, but they will never in themselves supply the relationship. Staring at a map of the United States will never project you into a morning walk round Jenny Lake, though it may evoke memories of it, fill you with a longing to go or show you the direction in which to set out. But some words and ideas, like some maps, are just out-dated, and more misleading than useful if you try to navigate by them.

It is some such confusion between the rounded world of relation in which I stand and take my place and the flat projection of words and ideas in which I try to map it out, which causes the present misunderstanding about 'God-language.' You said to me, just half-an-hour ago over supper: 'I sometimes think words should never have been invented — they never say what you mean.' It is for this same reason, I think, that some of us are finding it more and more difficult to talk without awkwardness about God. It is not because he is less real for us, but because he makes himself known 'in a relation that gathers up and includes all others,' as the true *Thou* of our life. We cannot therefore talk about him without making him, at the lowest, the object of our attention and, at best, *a* Person, a *Thou* among other *Thous*. Neither of these is what we would mean.

Is it then impossible to say anything? Buber is the first to recognize that words must be used. 'Many men wish to reject the word God as a legitimate usage, because it is so misused. It is indeed the most heavily laden of all the words used by men. For that very reason it is the most imperishable and most indispensable.' 'But all God's names are hallowed, for in them he is not merely spoken about, but also spoken to.'

The sad thing is that we are all of us lacking in tenderness for each other; we seem unwilling or unable to recognize that our neighbour meets his 'eternal *Thou*' through the particular 'name' he gives to

God. The 'believer' judges me a hypocrite because I cannot believe God is *a* Person, though I use language that seems to imply that I do; I judge the 'believer' credulous for making God an object of belief in an illusory supernatural world and thereby distorting him. Buber, with much tenderness, puts us all in our place: 'For he who speaks the word God and really has *Thou* in mind (whatever the illusion by which he is held) addresses the true *Thou* of his life, which cannot be limited by another *Thou*, and to which he stands in a relation that gathers up and includes all others. But when he, too, who abhors the name, and believes himself to be godless, gives his whole being to addressing the *Thou* of his life, as a *Thou* that cannot be limited by another, he addresses God.'

What may be said then about *Thou:* the *Thou* of the Italian peasant telling her beads at a village Mass, the *Thou* of the Buddhist monk devoting his life to the rehabilitation of the ex-Untouchables, the *Thou* of the doctor called out in the middle of the night or the scientist working late at his lab.? What can I say of the *Thou* of my life?

When I put down the book at the end of that afternoon, Buber had both helped me to see how I *could* perhaps say something of *Thou*, and taught me that I can after all say nothing, for even in speaking I destroy the *Thou* I speak of. I began to understand this dis-

comforting inability to talk about God because, as you
said, ' the words just don't say what you mean,' and
to see that the point at which I cease to be able to speak
is the point where I stand on the frontier of language
and step over into the world of relation. ' We speak
the primary word with our being, though we cannot
utter *Thou* with our lips.' To be unable to speak is not
to lose one's faith but to find one's trust; it is to know
oneself held by God who ' cannot be inferred in anything — in nature, say, as its author, or in history as its
master, or in the subject as the self that is thought in
it,' but who ' may properly only be addressed, not expressed.'

Buber had helped me to understand more also of
this twofold aspect of the world which produces the
effect of double vision. I am able to glimpse for myself
the elusive mystery of the world of relation in ' the
graciousness of its comings and the solemn sadness of
its goings.' I can accept for myself the claim laid upon
us to love the real world ' really in its horror ' in the
trust that ' if only we venture to surround it with the
arms of our spirit, our hands will meet hands that grip
them.' For I understand in my own life that ' without
It man cannot live. But he who lives with *It* alone is
not a man.'

I have, then, been given a diagnosis of my double vision, which up to now has caused me to bristle a little

uneasily at the taunts of others; though all along I have instinctively known it would be, for me, a greater disability to see with only one eye. But if my world is twofold, as Buber suggests, then my vision must also be twofold. The image of the *I–Thou* world of relation will be superimposed on the flat image of the *I–It* world of people and objects exterior to myself, giving it depth and perspective and value. If, however, I see God only through the *I–It* lens, believing in him, talking about him, experiencing him, my vision will no doubt be clear but without dimension. If I acknowledge and discern him through the lens of *Thou* but fear the image may be distorted or annihilated by the world of *It*, I shall be afraid to focus both lenses together and shall withdraw from the world. But if I live freely and joyfully in the world of *It*, welcoming it and loving it with tenderness and compassion, knowing that moment by moment, any person, any object, any purpose, may meet me as my *Thou*, then I shall be able to see clearly and in depth. One world will continuously be shot through by the other, and in all my fleeting daily *Thous* I shall be met and claimed by the eternal *Thou* of my life.

Nor will I so easily be confused by language, for I shall be able to use and value it as the natural currency in its own world, the world of *It*. It may indeed secure my passage to the very borders of the

world of *Thou*, so that I may say ' Abba, Father! ' as
the child says ' I love Teddy.' But it will buy me nothing from the world of *Thou*. It will neither enable me
to cross the border into direct relation nor secure that
relation for me in the world of *It*. I can never go on
to say ' Abba, Father! Therefore God *is* Father.' For
God ' may properly only be addressed not expressed.'

2

FOCUS ON CHRIST

IT IS important to be able to discern when the world of *Thou* is in question and when the world of *It*, above all when talking about Christ. For whereas God the eternal *Thou* can only be directly encountered in the world of *Thou*, Jesus, because he was a human being, belongs like me to both worlds. At no point is it more necessary to have my lenses in focus.

Sooner or later I am pinned down to the question: ' What think ye of Christ? ' Is he unique, divine, the Son of God, sinless? Did he exist before all time and is he alive with us now? To all these questions a Christian is expected to be able in some sense to answer a whole-hearted ' Yes.' ' Hold to Christ and, for the rest, be totally uncommitted ' leaves me, rather, asking myself: ' Am I really a Christian at all? '

Let us consider first the ' Christ event ' as a whole. By this I mean the birth of Jesus on the human scene and his impact on human history. Was this event unique? Here I find myself wondering what it means to describe an event as unique, except to say that every event is unique and unrepeatable, simply because it has happened. It is surely not that *a* divine Person is poking his finger into human affairs and making momentous decisions to set things right when they are in a mess. This is to relegate God to the world of *It*. To infer God from history is to cheapen both God and history and to take neither seriously.

Nor can we isolate an event from what went before or what comes after; an event has no hard edges. Some events are momentous because they come upon their hour; the world is, as it were, ready for them and seizes upon them with recognition. The significance of such an event lies as much in its repercussions as in its immediate historical context.

We have recently had an example of this on a more trivial level in the *Honest to God* event. In one sense this was simply a man using the opportunity of enforced inactivity to share his thinking with others. Its significance was not that it was new and startling but precisely that it was not; it was recognized as belonging to a great undercurrent of thinking seething below the surface and waiting for a channel to open for it. There have been so many who have said: ' This speaks for me.'

It is in this sense of belonging that Jesus ' belonged ' to the age he was born in. He was expected and the world was ready for him. People said not only ' This man speaks for me too ' but ' This man *lives* for me.' Indeed, so close has been the identification that ' *for* me ' has tended to become ' *instead of* me ' and has led to many debased and sickening theories of atonement.

In what way, then, was the world ready for Christ? I am not concerned here with expectations externalized in the racial and ecclesiastical terms of a Messiah, but with the underground spiritual consciousness of man itself. Jung, in his essay, ' A Psychological Approach to the Trinity,' suggests that, both personally and collectively, man comes to the point when he must recognize his own sonship and be able to detach himself from the Father in order to stand in reciprocal relation to him. On the collective, spiritual level he has to emerge from the unreflecting, completely passive dependence on God or the gods and begin to recognize his own sphere of responsibility and response. To put it on its lowest level, he must stop believing his neighbour's evil eye has caused his sickness and think in terms of medicine, not witch-doctors; he must give up thinking that every time it thunders the gods are angry. For it is only when he is freed from this automatic, unquestioning dependence, that he is able consciously to enter into a direct relationship with God and meet him face to face. This corresponds, in Buber's terms, to an acknowledgment and acceptance of

the relationship of *I* to *Thou*.

Jung suggests that Jesus represents, historically and psychologically, the point where man is inescapably brought up against this question of his Sonship. In the Old Testament, God is seen as distant and awesome. His face cannot be seen, he cannot even be named and men may not approach his holy mountain. In Jesus, the question of Sonship is brought to a head and resolved. It had to happen in the sense that, collectively or personally, the issue cannot be avoided.

It is interesting at this point to notice how hard we do try to avoid it. Christians still seem to be doing their best to foist the responsibilities of Sonship entirely on to Christ. We talk about him bearing the sin of the world, meaning that he took on the whole load himself in order to let us out. He did take on the ' whole load,' in the sense that he accepted for himself not only that man is responsible for the state of the world, but that he can change and redeem it by loving it and forgiving it. But we can neither say that he took it on instead of us nor that he did so in order to make it possible for us to take it on. All we *can* say is that in him we see the implications of accepting Sonship and acknowledge that what holds for him must hold for us.

In this context, the story of the Prodigal Son is significant for me, though I do not mean to suggest that this was the point of the parable as recorded in the Gospel. But it seems to me to be of the nature of a parable that it has a life of its own, not necessarily limited to a particular interpretation. It constantly forces one to stand inside it and listen afresh to what it may be saying. Let me then share with you what it has said to me about Sonship and the importunity of the claims of the Father. I have sometimes found myself wondering how long the returned wanderer managed to stick it out without making off again. His motives for coming back were entirely selfish and calculating — he would not have come if there had been any other way out of his economic difficulties. As it was, he was still hoping to be able to sit lightly to the family situation. 'I will set off and go to my father,' he thought to himself, 'and say to him, "Father, I have sinned against God and against you; I am no longer fit to be called your son; treat me as one of your paid servants."' In other words, he was hoping to stay on the fringe and not get too closely involved. But no such luck! As soon as he was in sight of home, there was the old boy smothering him as usual with love and affection and making such a 'thing' of it all. I can hardly think he enjoyed it any more than his brother did. What a pathetic family tragedy! One recognizes in the old man the irksome importunity of the widow claiming her rights, or the king organizing the party no one wanted to go to, and in the son the shrewdness of the bailiff who knew on which side his bread was buttered. This is a parable of sonship declined — not for me thank you! Neither brother had any love to offer the old man. The elder knew where his duty lay and the younger was only too glad to let him carry the can. Some Christians, in their turn, are relieved to think that Christ carries the can for them.

His life, on the contrary, is a parable of Sonship accepted. It expresses for us some of the deepest archetypal insights of the human spirit. Here, the conscious awareness of God as *Thou*, meeting Man with a direct personal claim, is seen to be openly acknowledged and accepted. Mind and spirit as it were join forces. Man's spirit is saved from having to go underground as a sort of resistance movement and is able instead to work out in the open, giving depth and dimension to his conscious rational existence. This is the ' event ' in Man's spiritual history which is pin-pointed in the Son-Father relationship acted out in the life of Jesus. As Jung puts it in his essay ' Answer to Job ': ' In this respect, he does in fact prove himself a σωτήρ, a Saviour. He preserves mankind from loss of communion with God and from getting lost in mere consciousness and rationality. That would have brought something like a dissociation between consciousness and the unconscious, an unnatural and even pathological condition, a " loss of soul " such as has threatened man from the beginning of time.'

Because his companions and followers were aware of this spiritual ' event ' as a happening of great moment involving the whole of humanity, the events of his life-time have, as it were, absorbed the ' rub-off ' of its spiritual significance. It is as if the communication-line of the *Thou* world of relation and the *It* world of history got crossed. Or, to put it another way, as if the ' events ' of the *Thou* world, in order to be communicated consciously, had to be translated and projected in the time and space scale of the *It* world, just as a natural landscape is projected on to a map. Perhaps we have just not known how to handle this sudden confrontation with the *Thou* world and have had to accommodate it to the familiar terms of the *It* world. We have not been able to recognize an entirely different mode of being.

And so it is that the natural events of Jesus' life have acquired a magical significance. Awareness of the decisive spiritual ' event ' of his life and its far-reaching implications associated the incident of his birth with extraordinary occurrences in the material world: spontaneous pregnancy, strange movements of the stars, the opening of the heavens and choirs of angels. After his death his immediate friends, drawn into this new mode of being during his life, were now joyfully aware of its power released among them, and interpreted the inner ' event ' in terms of the outward circumstances of his burial. Later, the process was reversed; the spiritual ' event ' was inferred from the circumstances of the burial and thereby dragged into the *It*-world of doctrine and belief.

Now if it were proved beyond doubt that Jesus were the illegitimate child of a human father or his bones were unmistakably identified in a Palestinian grave, this would make no difference to my commitment ' in Christ.' In fact it would clear out of the way many misconceptions and make the real claim on my own life less easy to escape. Such evidence is unlikely at the distance of two thousand years, but why be afraid to allow the possibility, or even the probability? Who is more likely than an illegitimate child, wondering who his real father was (' God is your real father, dear '), to be passionately concerned with the Father-Son relationship, especially if he is more than ordinarily intuitive and intellectually precocious? No doubt he gave his mother much to ponder in her heart. But whatever the circumstantial facts, the ' historicity ' of the Christian gospel for me lies deeper than that.

But this is not to answer ' No ' to the question: Do you believe in incarnation or resurrection? The theme of the son of the gods being born to a mortal woman and of his miraculous rebirth is one that recurs many times in many cultures. It is one of those threads of archetypal ' knowledge ' or perceptiveness which link us to the source of all our being. We may in one sense be ' come of age,' but in another we are still in the womb, dependent on the umbilical cord that safeguards our full and potential humanity. Perceptions of incarnation and resurrection are threads in that cord and represent real factors in our existence.

We can no longer, however, limit these concepts to external events, however apposite these events may be for us as symbols. It always seems to me that the Roman Catholic church is in this regard in a much stronger position than the other churches who have compromised and distinguished between what is ' historical ' and what is not. There is really no difference in kind between the dogmas of the Immaculate Conception and Assumption of Mary, and the dogmas of the Virgin Birth and Ascension of Christ. One day we shall wake up to find a Vatican Council has openly spelt out the spiritual function of dogma and we shall be left ' holding the baby ' and trying to explain a historical Virgin Birth!

We may say, then, to sum up thus far, that the ' uniqueness ' of the historical event of Jesus is that there is here acted out, in terms of a human existence, a spiritual ' event ' in the unconscious being of Mankind, namely the bringing to consciousness of Man's relation to his eternal *Thou*.

But what of the man himself, this particular man Jesus? How does uniqueness apply to him? I find it easier to start by asking how he is unique or, at any rate, ' special ' for me. He is special for me as he takes his stand ' within relation,' in Buber's sense. My commitment is to the *I* of the Son as he meets the *Thou* of the Father, for this is where I too would stand.

But Buber has shown us that the *I* of *I–Thou* is different from the *I* of *I–It*, so it is not to the individual, the man called Jesus of Nazareth, that I am committed. Such a man is unknown to me. It is true that a picture of him has been built up in my mind from various sources, but this is largely imaginary and unverifiable. I can never know for myself what he was like as a person, nor am I really concerned to know, apart from natural curiosity. I have no more to do with an individual who lived 2000 years ago than he with me.

Nor am I committed to an extension of this individual backwards or forwards in time, either as someone who has always existed or as a ghostly figure hovering at my back watching my every move.

Theologians have sometimes tried to distinguish between the Jesus of history and the Christ of faith, but this is a false distinction for me. My commitment is to the *I* of Jesus claimed by and responding to the *Thou* of the Father, caught up within the relation in which he takes his stand. He is for me the man who most clearly puts in focus the twofold world in which I live. It is he who shows most dynamically the impact of the one world upon the other, revealing at once their interdependence and their incompatibility. Here I shudder before the awful implications of standing truly in relation, as *I* to *Thou* in every encounter of my life.

I should like to consider in some detail, by way of illustration, a conversation recorded in the Fourth Gospel (Chapter 8) between Jesus and the Pharisees in Jerusalem.

Jesus begins by saying: ' I am the light of the world. No follower of mine shall wander in the dark; he shall have the light of life.' Now if we understand this *I* to be spoken, as it were, with the whole being, by the *I* of Jesus responding to his *Thou*, and not by the *I* of self-consciousness, separation and individuality, the whole conversation indeed takes on a new light. What Jesus is saying can then be translated something like this: ' The *I* of the whole being related to its *Thou* is the whole meaning of existence. No one who follows me and takes his stand in this relation *I–Thou* will be in despair or without purpose; his whole life will light up with meaning.'

This theme is very close to the heart of the Fourth Gospel and is indeed the note on which it opens:

' When all things began, the Word (*I–Thou*) already
was. The Word dwelt with God, and what God was,
the Word was. (That is to say, the component parts
of *I–Thou* can never be split; when the *I* of relation
is spoken, the whole relation *I–Thou* is involved. Or,
to put it another way: ' I and the Father are one.') The
Word, then, was with God at the beginning, and
through him all things came to be; no single thing was
created without him. (There is nothing outside the
scope of *I–Thou*; ' Thou-ness ' is implicit, as it were,
in the whole of life.) All that came to be was alive
with his life, and that life was the light of men. (As
Buber would say: ' All real living is meeting.') The
light shines on in the dark, and the darkness has never
quenched it. (The world of relation can never be absorbed — or understood in terms of — the world of
It.) '

In their conversation, Jesus and the Pharisees are
speaking on two entirely different levels: Jesus speaks
the *I* of *I–Thou* and his hearers imply the *I* of *I–It*, that
is, the individual standing before them. Jesus is, in
fact, attempting to communicate across the frontier of
language. It leads to utter confusion. ' The word *I* is
the true shibboleth of mankind,' says Buber: as in the
original story in Judges 12, it shows a man up for what
he really is. They complain that his witness is invalid
because he is pleading his own cause, but Jesus claims

it *is* valid, even though he is speaking about himself, ' because I know where I come from, and where I am going '; that is, he understands the relation in which he stands when he speaks this *I*.

The Pharisees ask him: ' Where is your father? ' His answer is: ' You neither know me nor my Father; if you knew me you would know my Father as well.' That is: ' If you were aware that it is the *I* of *I–Thou* who speaks, you would recognize the *Thou* by whom *I* am claimed.'

Later he says: ' I am revealing in words what I saw in my Father's presence (trying to communicate in words what is beyond language and can only be known in relation); and you are revealing in action what you learned from your father (showing by the sort of people you are, the cash-value of the doctrines you have inherited). Why do you not understand my language? It is because my revelation is beyond your grasp.' Of course it is! The world of relation can never be possessed in any sense; it can never be neatly buttoned up in the mind, but only ' known ' by the whole being standing within it. Any language about it is never more than a hint.

Jesus then goes on to say: ' It is the Father who glorifies me, he of whom you say: " He is our God " (the object of your belief), though you do not know him (as your *Thou*).' ' Your father Abraham was overjoyed to see my day; he saw it and was glad.' Abraham, that is, knew what it was to be claimed by *Thou* and to answer as the *I* within relation.

This, then, is the context of the much-debated: ' In very truth I tell you, before Abraham was born, I am.' The Pharisees can only understand him to be speaking the *I* of the individual and to be asserting the precedence of this *I*. The point, however, is not that Jesus existed before Abraham did, but that the *I* within *I–Thou* is always the *primary* response of man to the *Thou* who claims him. This is true both of the emerging human race and the growing personality. What precisely Jesus consciously meant (in the intellectual sense) when he spoke these words, or what the writer of the Fourth Gospel understood in putting them on his lips, is one factor, but not the only one, to be considered. For when a man is able to speak directly from his inner being, with archetypal intuition of our common destiny, he is apt to say more than he knows at the surface of his mind. (This is also true of a painter in relation to his art.)

But the Pharisees, listening to these words, take aim to destroy this man, this individual standing before them, by hurling in his teeth the sharp, lifeless arguments of theological dogmatism. Such weapons, however, are useless when it is the *I* of relation under attack. Of this *I* they are simply not aware. In the pregnant words with which the chapter ends: 'They picked up stones to throw at him, but Jesus was not to be seen.'

This also is the 'light' in which we can understand the parables 'if we have ears to hear.' It is the nature of a parable, a tale or a fairy story to have meaning on many different levels. It is a question of where the hearer takes his stand. The Sleeping Beauty means something very different for the child and the psychiatrist; the fascination the story holds for both, and the persistence and recurrence of the theme, is an indication that we are all more deeply involved within the story than we know. The Zen and Sufi masters who teach by means of tales do not involve themselves in interpretation; the meaning can only be known by the pupil himself as he puts himself in the way of it.

So it is with the New Testament stories told by Jesus. 'He who has ears to hear, let him hear.' The *I* who is claimed by *Thou* will hear differently from the *I* cudgelling my brains to understand the allusions.

Consider some of the parables about the Kingdom. The Kingdom of Heaven is not to be taken as another world, in the sense of a life after this one or separate from this one, but as another mode of being in which I take my stand 'in relation.' 'The world which appears to you in this way,' says Buber, 'is unreliable, for it takes on a continually new appearance ' (a grain of mustard, leaven, a fig-tree); ' you cannot hold it to its word.' And indeed, how often the parables seem to be taking a rise out of us: the master actually commending the unjust steward, the man condemned for not having a wedding garment, the irascible old judge settling a case, not from any sense of right, but simply to get a bit of peace. St Luke found them a bit too uncomfortable at times and took to adding a few tamely pious words of explanation to tone them down. But importunity is a characteristic of the world of *Thou* (' Go out on to the highways and along the hedgerows and make them come in '); it comes even when it is not summoned (the thief in the night) and vanishes even when it is tightly held (the buried talent).

This, then, is the context in which the New Testament gospel speaks to me, in Christ, as ' good news.' It is also the context in which I understand the ' Christ that dwelleth in me.' It is not that I am invaded by an invisible Presence, personified as an extension of Christ's human personality, who is thinking my thoughts or acting as my conscience. Rather is it that I am called by the *Thou* who claimed him, to speak the *I* he spoke and to speak this *I* with my whole being. ' This is my beloved Son ' claims this *I* from the depths of *my* being and calls *me* into living sonship.

But just as the significance of the spiritual ‘ event ’ of Jesus Christ has ‘ rubbed off ’ on to the external occurrences of his life, so has the spiritual significance of his *I*-in-relation ‘ rubbed off ’ on to his individual personality. His one-ness with the Father, his claim to be sent by the Father, has been projected on to a flat map of divinity for all to observe, and translated into a lifeless schedule of sinlessness for all to admire. The result is that his true humanity has been missed. He has become a semi-magical, ethereal figure, not really belonging to this world but lent to it for a season. Such a man lays no claim upon me, nor do I feel one. His *true* humanity, the humanity to which we are all called, lay in his unbounded readiness to speak the *I* of relation, to respond to his *Thou* in all the daily encounters of his life, even when it meant death. He said ‘ Yes ’ to life with his whole being, accepting and forgiving the world about him, constantly healing and renewing it wherever the Word was spoken.

Such a man does claim me. I take my stand alongside him not in belief but in trust. I cannot say I believe in a personal Being called God, nor can I say I believe that Jesus was the Son of this God. These statements belong to the world of *It* where God and Christ remain objects of my belief. But in any encounter of my life, personal or social, intellectual or artistic, important or trivial, I know I am required to take my stand in trust, wholly committed, holding nothing back, ready to meet and be met by a hundred daily *Thous* and, through them, to encounter the eternal, unqualified *Thou* of my life that hounds me ' down the arches of the years.'

There is no proof that this is the meaning, purpose and destiny of life. I simply live within this trust and can no other.

3

LIVING IN THE SPIRIT

I SHALL find this section of my ' letter ' by far the most difficult to write as it is all much nearer the bone. So far I have tried to give you some idea of Buber's concept of the world of relation, and to show how this lights up the difference between meeting God as *Thou* and talking about ' Him ' as a Person. Then I have described how, for me, this mode, or ' Way,' to use a biblical phrase, of human response is brought to life in Christ. Now I must try and talk about how we can actually *live* in this ' Way ' and be in this world of relation ourselves.

Being ' in relation ' corresponds to what the New Testament calls ' living in the Spirit.' Buber says that spirit is ' between *I* and *Thou*. It is not like the blood that circulates in you, but like the air in which you breathe. Man lives in the spirit, if he is able to respond to his *Thou*. He is able to, if he enters into relation with his whole being. Only in virtue of his power to enter into relation is he able to live in the Spirit.' The community of Holy Spirit is the reciprocal encounter of those who are mutually held in this relation of total claim and response, whether or not it is recognized consciously or verbally. Indeed, recognition tends to come afterwards as a sort of postscript to the encounter, like the photograph of an event that has already happened.

The Emmaus story (Luke 24) brings to life such an encounter ' in the Spirit.' Whether or not the two friends actually met a third person on the road we cannot know and it doesn't matter. The story is ' true ' in the sense that we *know* it to be true, for this is just how it goes in our own experience. As they opened their hearts to each other, sharing their doubts and fears and hopes, and offering to each other the comfort of their shared need, a fire was kindled between them, a living spark which held them enthralled. As each *I* met and responded to the *Thou* of the other, that same spirit was between them that had linked the *I* of Jesus to the *Thou* of his Father, and each was able to speak this *I* for himself. The *I* of Jesus was with them on the way.

The moment of mutual recognition at the supper table is one we know for ourselves. You are just passing the bread, you catch the other person's eye, and in that moment of awareness the thread breaks and the moment freezes. The act becomes self-conscious and you become separate individuals again; what was between you is lost but you recognize what it is you have shared and lost. 'Then their eyes were opened, and they recognized him; and he vanished from their sight.'

Do you know Rupert Brooke's 'Dining Room Tea'? This poem is always linked with the Emmaus story for me: the one always reminds me of the other. Both try to recapture that frozen moment when the world of relation breaks upon the consciousness and time stands still:

> I saw the marble cup; the tea,
> Hung on the air, an amber stream;
> I saw the fire's unglittering gleam,
> The painted flame, the frozen smoke.

until time begins to creep again and the scene once more comes to life:

> Light glinted on the eyes I loved.
> The cup was filled. The bodies moved.
> The drifting petal came to ground
> The laughter chimed its perfect round.
> The broken syllable was ended.

How can I ever communicate what lies between the pouring of the tea and the filling of the cup, ' or shake at time's sufficient spell, stammering of lights unutterable?.' I only know that I have met the claim of another over against me; I have known ' the eternal holi-

ness of you ' and meeting *Thou* in you, have found my true identity as *I*.

This, for me, is something of what happened on the way to Emmaus and in the moment of recognition at supper. And it helps me to understand what is meant by the words spoken by Jesus in the Fourth Gospel: ' It is for your good that I am leaving you. If I do not go, your Advocate will not come, whereas if I go, I will send him to you.' The *I* that had to go was the *I* of the individual, the man on whom, during his lifetime, his followers had pinned all their hopes. As long as they clung to this *I*, like Mary in the garden clutching on to the tangible familiar form, they could never know in themselves the *I* of relation. When they knew this *I* to be alive in them, not buried with him, the world of *Thou* was open to them, and they found the whole created universe waiting, craning its neck, for their response.

It seems to be the tragedy of men that we always have difficulty in ' earthing ' our inner perceptions; the truer they are, the more impossible it is to give form to them. As Buber puts it, it is ' the exalted melancholy of our fate, that every *Thou* in our world must become an *It*.' And we generally bungle it. Our perception of God as ' *Thou* ' has been flattened out into a concept of a Divine Being. Our perception of the true *I* of man's response has become fixed in the individual identity of Jesus. Our perception of the 'fellowship' in which *I* and *Thou* are related has likewise been fossilized into the structure of the Religious Organization.

Our problem is to distinguish between the fellowship of the Spirit and this ecclesiastical structure, to recognize that they sometimes overlap but not always, and to assess at any moment which is the prior allegiance and where it claims us. 'The *It* (the structure) is the eternal chrysalis, the *Thou* (the fellowship) the eternal butterfly — except that situations do not always follow one another in clear succession, but often there is a happening profoundly twofold, confusedly entangled.' It is this 'confusedly entangled' situation that we must now try and sort out.

That the life of the Spirit cuts across the boundaries of the Religious Organization has been implicit from the beginning. In St Paul's day it was a question of whether you had to be circumcised to be a Christian. Now it is rather a question of whether you have to be religious to be 'in the Spirit.' Jesus himself was the first to make the point that what matters is meeting commitment, not defining it: 'Not everyone who calls me "Lord, Lord" will enter the kingdom of Heaven, but only those who do the will of my heavenly Father.' There are many today who are feeding the hungry, healing the sick and visiting the fatherless and widows who do not think of what they do in terms of

Christ. They do it not because they are Christians but because people are hungry and sick and lonely.

Nor is the Spirit confined to social action. ' Man speaks with many tongues, tongues of language, of art, of action; but the spirit is one, the response to the *Thou* which appears and addresses him out of the mystery.' The poet, the artist, the scientist, each in his sphere, where he is wholly committed with nothing withheld, is ' in the Spirit.' The poet puts into words, the artist into paint or stone, the scientist follows through to the last equation, whatever is claimed from him as he says ' Yes ' to his *Thou*.

The function of the Church, as an organization, is to act as a vehicle for this life of the Spirit, to body it forth in the world. When it doesn't do that it is an empty shell. It is the function of the Church to point the way and blaze the trail, not to set our feet in concrete as we tread the road.

Many things initiated by the Church have now passed outside the ' religious ' sphere altogether. In the Middle Ages, the Church was the main patron of music and drama and art. Mystery and morality plays were performed on church premises, music was composed for church services, and paintings and sculpture commissioned to adorn church buildings. Today we have theatres and concert halls specially built for the purpose, where there is more active ' washing away of sin,' in the sense that the Greeks well understood, than in many church services.

In the social sphere also, reforms in the nineteenth century were prompted by the Christian conscience, and the Church led the way in building hospitals and schools and launching societies to further social welfare. Today the State has rightly accepted these responsibilities and gradually more amenities are within the reach of every citizen. All this is good and as it should be; a matter for real gladness, not despair. What a tragedy that the Church should often cling so tenaciously to what it fosters, whether church schools or church societies, in the mood of '*they* will take them over if we don't watch out.' The Church is the servant of society, not its rival, and should concentrate its resources on showing what is the best that can be done, be glad when its pioneering jobs are taken over, and then turn its energies to the next thing in hand.

The Church is fearful for its structure, for its structure is decaying; of that there is no doubt. But this again is as it should be if the Spirit is alive and active. For where the Spirit is, there is nothing set or fixed, rigid or permanent. Where the Spirit is, all is flux. In a community of the Spirit, no group or movement, whether church organization or local congregation, should be so welded that it cannot be disbanded when the Spirit outgrows it and seeks some other form. We think too much of form and structure for its own sake and too little of the community it is built for. If the Church really takes seriously its identity as the body of Christ it must remember what happened to that body, and be prepared to accept death, whenever necessary, in order that new life may be possible. It must not cling to the old forms and the old structures but let them go, and run to the brethren with news of the Spirit let loose in the world.

But the ecclesiastical structure has become, alas, a vast crumbling depository of latent fears and hopes, of guilt and good intentions, of avoided relationships or moments of truth, all stacked up behind a fine Gothic façade. Behind this frontage, both those who are church attenders and those who stay away can reassure themselves that their vital concerns are being attended to and that business is being carried on as usual.

I may have a new baby and want to give him the best possible start in life. So he has all his protective inoculations and, because I realize there are spiritual as well as bodily hazards, I take him into church for a dash of Holy Spirit. But a splash of water in itself will give him nothing except perhaps a fright. Only in his growing relationship with me and others at home will he learn to love and trust, to give and take forgiveness, to be a whole person. So it is no good leaving his spiritual needs wrapped up in a parcel on the font addressed to the Church.

I may have a beautiful white wedding with several bridesmaids and the choir — and a husband thrown in. But it is no good leaving my promises in a wedding-cake box on the altar rail addressed to my husband for he will never find them there. He will only find them in what I am to him day by day as I meet him in loving, open encounter face to face at home.

I may kneel in my pew, Sunday by Sunday, spilling out my resentments and my hopes, my hatreds and my loves, but it is useless to leave them there in a pile addressed to sender. I have to take them home and work them out openly and honestly in the relationships to which they belong, even when it means exposing myself to hurt and rejection. But the Church is piled high with our parcels, discarded and unopened for there is no one there to open them, while our world at home gasps for the lack of what they could provide.

The gift of the Spirit which enables us to say *Thou* is not a talent to be buried for safety in the crypt, nor a coin to be shown in a glass case on Sunday (with Gothic inscription in King James English). It is everyday currency for spending in the world. It belongs to the world and not to the Church, and the Church should give up trying to appropriate the funds, for it has no monopoly of Holy Spirit. It should rather be a trusted accountant, helping the world to invest and spend its spiritual resources wisely and well.

If then the function of the ecclesiastical organization is to be a servant in the world's household, what of the living organism, the community of the Spirit, and of our stand within it? How do Spirit and structure overlap? This is the point where many of us today feel torn and divided. I said before that the community of the Spirit is the reciprocal encounter of those who are mutually held in a relation of total claim and response. But because we are flesh and blood and not disembodied spirits, it is also the bodying forth, the incarnation, of that encounter in terms of this world's relationships. When I say I believe in incarnation this is what I mean — my neighbour meeting me with the claim of *Thou*.

This community of Holy Spirit, this ' fellowship ' (in the New Testament, not the ' fishy hand-clasp,' sense) is no visible society you can decide to join. It is no question of membership cards or counting heads; you cannot automatically enrol for life. But sometimes you will know that you are ' in,' it may be with friends or total strangers; it is a question of being able to ' discern the body ' and know yourself a member of it. This body is a continuously shifting kaleidoscope of pieces re-arranging themselves in overlapping patterns — its outward form is never still. It may be a civil rights march, a Quaker meeting, a conversation in a train, but it is just as likely to take a much less respectable and conventional form than any of these. There is nothing necessarily ' religious ' about its appearance.

' Discerning the body ' is the particular ministry of the Christian in society, for in taking his stand with Christ he is accepting *consciously* the claim of *Thou* upon him and laying himself open to meet and respond to it however it may come. It is a ministry of caring — of caring about people and of human values, and about all that deepens and widens our perception, whether in art or science. It is a ministry of saying ' Yes ' to life in trust and hope. Such a ministry is not at all concerned with working upon people to persuade, cajole or exhort them in the sense of: ' You need what I've got. Open your mouth and swallow and see how much better you feel.' It can only be undertaken by those who have the grace to accept from others the ministry they themselves offer — the invitation to say *Thou* with honesty and compassion and, in saying it, to find the true identity of *I*.

This then is the primary aspect of the ministry of a Christian in the world: to take his stand with Christ in conscious acceptance of the claim of *Thou*. But he must also stand with other Christians in providing, as Christ did, a focus between the two aspects of our world, that of relation and that of external forms, so that the world is seen rounded and whole, and not simply in the flat dimension of space-time.

There is the constant temptation to ask why we have to have outward forms of realities that can never adequately be expressed. Why do we have to have services and sacraments? Is an ecclesiastical structure necessary at all? But since the beginning of time, man has found that he needs to act out in some form those perceptions that he cannot otherwise communicate. Even ordinary gestures like waving or cheering, a handshake or a pat on the back, are shorthand actions for a whole complex of feelings and attitudes which we are able in this way to bring to the surface and communicate. The action itself is understood as self-explanatory. But the deeper and more complex our perceptions, the more corporate and universal they are, the greater the urgency for some outward form of expression to release the tension they create. Religious ritual provides at a corporate level the same sort of shorthand that personal gestures provide at the level of the individual. As in the theatre, it attempts to bring spiritual happenings down to the scale of the capacity of the human imagination. The only requirement is that the outward action should be forced out of us by the inner compulsion and not be performed to cover up its lack. There is some ritual that represents at the spiritual level what the forced smile, the polite clap

or the dandy's flourish represents at the level of personal feeling, and this should be exposed and disowned.

As you know, we have felt for ourselves in our own family this doubt about outward forms and symbols. Our weekly Family Supper, at which we have tried to express for ourselves at the domestic level what Communion represents in church, has become a very movable feast, and where it is taking us we just don't know. One voice among us says: ' Why can't we just enjoy being all together without having to talk about anything special? ' Another voice says: ' But you have to have a point where you can gather everything together and share in the open what lies on the inside. If you don't, the inside withers away in the dark.' Somewhere between these two we are trying to feel our way. But one thing is certain. There is no point at which we can stop and say: ' This is it. This is how it should be. This is how we'll always do it,' because the next time it will just be ' the thing to do ' and go dead on us. We are like gypsies, continually being moved on.

This, I think, is a pattern of how liturgy should move and grow in the Church. We do need a point at which we can gather everything together, but it mustn't be so rigid or fixed that it has no flexibility to move with a living, changing community. Liturgy must be kept alive and fluid, taking whatever form it is forced into from within, for it is the life of the community alone which is the reason for its existence.

There will always, of course, be a residual pattern running through from generation to generation and bearing an accumulated weight of meaning which we can't let go, but the forms of this pattern will shift and change as the life of the community dictates.

We can see what happens when the forms and patterns of liturgy are *not* evolved naturally from the life of the community but imposed from above by the 'management.' A Liturgical Commission is appointed to juggle with the words and bring them more up-to-date, but it is guided primarily, not by what the Spirit demands, but by what theology permits. It is sympathetically aware of modern needs but in the way of concession not conviction. Its purpose in the last resort is to safeguard the structure, not to direct a breakthrough of the Spirit. This is not to say that such a Commission is a waste of time; at least it is the beginning of a softening-up process from the other end. But unless there is, at the same time, real freedom and encouragement to experiment in the Spirit at the local level, nothing will basically be changed.

As it is, we find at the local level that the community has to fit itself into the liturgical structure as into a strait-jacket with just as much discomfort and restriction. The connection between Communion and

Confirmation, for example, is a harmful anomaly. Confirmation is an adult commitment and should not be expected from children and adolescents. The wrong questions are continually being asked. The age at which any particular child should be admitted to Communion cannot be assessed by asking ' Has he been confirmed?,' but by asking: ' What does his share in the life of the community require? What seems good to the Holy Spirit and to us? ' And the same anomalies occur when questions of intercommunion between the denominations arise at the local level.

But the greatest farce of all in this subordination of the life of the Spirit to the structure in which it is confined is in the consecration of buildings and property, which sets them apart for ever and prevents their use for any ' common ' purpose even when it is for the common good of the community. This is where magic takes over and the whole system falls into disrepute. How can it claim our commitment?

Just as we are having to feel our way at the domestic level in asking how or whether we can ever express the inwardness of a shared reality in a recognized outward form, so it is in the wider community of the Spirit. The answer is that we just don't know. It seems that the very moment of finding a form to express the inwardness is the point at which the inwardness vanishes. Our *Thou* is continually becoming an *It*. Nevertheless, we know that the whole of life is a search for a form, an expression, and the search is forced upon us from within; we cannot relinquish it. We are all alchemists, committed to the discovery of the philosopher's stone, though we know it will never be available to us as a hard tangible substance to hold in the hand. But there are, alas, many practitioners working on the assumption that it will.

The same question mark is poised over the structure of the ecclesiastical organization as over the structure of its liturgy. Whether or in what form an ' organization ' of the Spirit is possible or necessary, we can only say we don't know. We are only sure that there can be no blue-print available in advance and that it would be a structure continually moving and changing. We are certain that it must change from what it is now, and that it must change from below if it is to do so in any life-giving way. Change from above by the management will be merely theoretical and, on its own, irrelevant.

There are signs of a breakthrough. We are at last beginning to think of ' ministry ' in terms of the Christian's service to the world for the world's own sake rather than of the priest's authority over the layman for the Church's sake. Young men are committing themselves to try and discover what the role of an ordained priest or minister may be within this ministry.

Groups of people are meeting here and there to find out for themselves what it means for the Church to be gathered together in one place, in an age when the parish system is decreasingly relevant to the social structure in which we live. Christians in this place and that are rediscovering their calling to provide an accepting, forgiving and reconciling community, often cutting across the boundary of religious commitment and practice or even without reference to it at all.

But ministry at ground level, which is the only level where it can be any use, is often conflicting and bewildering, and it is here that we need to be able to allow in ourselves the same flexibility and openness that we demand from the ecclesiastical organization.

You and I may belong to many different sorts of groups and communities which are continually overlapping and changing, and it so often seems to be the most ' secular ' and non-religious groups that offer the freedom and the challenge to meet, and respond to, a shared *Thou*. We easily recognize for ourselves which these are. Sometimes the local parish organization may be such a group, but what if it isn't? What if we are asking ourselves just how much longer we can go on attending church services Sunday by Sunday? It is then that we feel torn between boredom and obligation, between exasperation with the structure and tenderness for the people who are actually *there*, some needing so much, others with so much to give and share.

It seems to me that in this situation we have to walk freely ' in the Spirit,' neither shrugging off responsibility for the local congregation, nor being swallowed up by it. Our relation to it shouldn't be allowed to drain all our resources so that we have nothing to offer elsewhere, like a dutiful spinster daughter whose life is eaten up by the emotional demands of an ageing parent. If we go to church services or take part in parish activities, we have to give gladly whatever we can, within the given framework and with the help of whatever spiritual translation we may personally need to make for it to be real for us. And if Sunday by Sunday is too much for our staying-power, if our real re-creation in the Spirit lies elsewhere, let us at least stay away joyfully and to some purpose, so that when we *are* part of the local congregation we have something to give and share.

What we *can* give, how we are able to give it and at what points we are most built up in the Spirit will be different for each of us, and indeed will always be changing according to the constant flux of our external commitments and relationships. For some of us, our ministry lies mainly outside the ecclesiastical organization and the religious sphere, helping the world to recapture the depth and dimension of the world of

Thou. For others it is mainly within the religious structure, building up a living liturgy through which this depth and dimension can be expressed and shared.

Most of us move continually across this frontier, partly outside partly inside, some more out than in. As we do so we rejoice to note how well-trodden the whole area is becoming and how increasingly difficult it is to know precisely where the line is actually drawn. Militant churchmen and militant atheists are in no doubt; they never come within miles of the border anyhow. But for those of us on the fringe on either side, it is a frontier we can well do without for it has ceased to have any significance. Our first commitment is to the Spirit, whichever way the wind is blowing.

POSTSCRIPT

SO THERE it is, 'my fair pretty maid'! It is seventeen years ago that you were born, right in the heart of the Establishment, behind the medieval stonework of Vicars' Close and under the shadow of Wells Cathedral. The following day you lay in your pram in a warm patch up against St Catherine's chapel where you were later baptized. The canons and theological students passed you at regular intervals on their way up and down to matins, sext, evensong — pausing to observe this new intrusion on the familiar scene.

Your early days were measured out between the jousting knights on the cathedral clock at noon and the bishop's swans tugging at their bell for food at four. One of your first remembered traumatic experiences was caused by a friendly ordinand playfully flapping his black gown at you on his way up the Close; for months you would turn and bury your face against the sink whenever he appeared in the kitchen.

Now you are no longer at home in the Close, sheltered by the huge bulk of the cathedral from the noise of the traffic in the market place beyond; you are out there in the traffic that invades the cloister with disruptive echoes of a working day. Your timetable is determined no longer by clockwork knights and hungry swans, but by alarm clocks and school bells, telephones and door-bells.

You may think perhaps there is some loss in that, but the gain is incomparably greater. And the greatest gain of all is knowing that life is not after all a choice between the cold, material reassurance of the kitchen sink and that other-worldly spookiness wrapped round in its black theological gown. For you have learned to turn round and face that flapping disembodied sleeve and to see through it to the flesh and blood inside, to the living human hand that reaches out to claim your own in love and trust.

And now, to end this birthday letter on a gay note, here is an additional unofficial verse for your song, to be sung, let's say, *in Spiritu:*

> How will you live, my fair pretty maid?
> How will you live, my honey?
> She answered me right cheerfully:
> I'll live it up come Sunday!
> With my rue dum day, fol the diddle dol,
> Fol the dol the diddle dum the day.

ABOUT THE AUTHOR

RUTH ROBINSON is a graduate of Cambridge University where she read the Modern Languages Tripos and took First Class Honours in Spanish and French.

It was at Cambridge that she met John A. T. Robinson, now Bishop of Woolwich. They were married in 1947 and have four children. Catherine is the second in the family and the eldest of the three girls.